WHEN CHERRY
BLOSSOMS BLOOM

Living with a Life-Limiting illness

By

Valarie Lovelight

Life is like the cherry blossom, as its span is brief. The tree's beautiful blooming flowers last only about two weeks before they start to wither and fall to the ground. We too are only here for a moment in time with some moments being shorter than others, but all moments come to an end. When we look at how long the Earth has existed, our life in comparison is short, like the cherry blossom. So, let's give off a beautiful fragrance of love, hope, joy, and peace for others to remember us by.

Living life to the fullest has nothing to do with material things and everything to do with what we pour out onto others—love!

The Cherry Blossoms of Life!

The delightful fragrance of life so sweet.

Draws me to you, a life so brief.

As your petals start to fall,

They do it with grace.

Drifting down on wings of love.

Tears fall as one brushes my face,

A gentle touch of love's embrace.

Kissing the ground, their final resting place.

New season, new bloom, memories so dear,

A beautiful reminder that you were here.

—Valarie Lovelight

Table of Contents

INTRODUCTION

A gentle breeze blows in winds of change. Sometimes the breeze can be soft and warm and at other times it harsh and cold. We do our best to prepare for changes even when we don't know what they are or when they will come. It's the same with death.

In life we are faced with so many challenges. All are significant because they can have us reflecting on or living in the past, disrupt our present and stifle our future. Because of this we must find the strength to navigate our way through a range of emotions that might come with it. Maintaining control as much as possible is important when dealing with situations that affect our relationships and quality of life.

Whenever we receive bad news, it can be devastating. Our mind tries to find a way to process the information while trying to protect us from a complete breakdown. Unfortunately, this doesn't always work. Our mind is like a canvas, and our imagination paints various pictures of worst-case scenarios, even if it's a natural part of life, like dying.

Death is a part of life. Dealing with it is something we all must do at some point in time. Unfortunately, dying is still hard to accept, think about, or even talk about. It's a natural part of life that we know is inevitable. The thought of dying or seeing our loved ones dying is an emotional battle. Letting go and continuing with our lives is not easy. Like sand slipping through our fingers, life at times can feel the same way, leaving behind only a memory of what once was.

Some cultures embrace death instead of fearing it. Loved ones who are dying are cared for and not seen as a burden. It is viewed as a natural part of the life cycle, the circle of life. Yet, here in America death is feared and not discussed in a positive or healthy way. Caring for loved ones, for many, is seen as a burden rather than an act of love, and people fall apart at the thought of it.

At that point, a helping hand maybe needed to make it through. Thankfully, there's so much information available to help survivors of loss cope. For example: support groups, counselors, and books written on dealing with grief that can help us navigate through the maze of emotions that follows loss. In time most people move on with their lives. The sun will one day shine, and the memories of loved ones will become less painful as people start to focus on the good times and not the loss.

However, what about those who have yet to die, who are suffering from an illness? Those who have received heart-wrenching news about a terminal illness that will limit their quality of life and could at some point end it? How are they coping? What emotions are they feeling? There are support groups to help them process and deal with the life-changing news, but, overall, most people outside those programs are clueless as to how to get the support they need.

It's when a family focuses on the thought of losing their loved one that grief starts to set in. Too often we allow the news of cancer, MS, AIDS, lupus, or dementia to cause us to neglect the person or treat them as though they have already died. Our grief can cause us to become so selfish and consumed that we forget about our loved ones and what they are going through.

In this book, my goal is to help us to be more focused and supportive to our terminally ill loved ones, as well as give insight on their thoughts and needs. Let grief take a backseat so that we can effectively help and cherish them while making the most of the time we have with them.

A few years ago, I started jotting down notes when my father told me they found polyps in his colon. Although he has other health challenges, he is okay and being monitored. But at one point he broke down and cried over the phone, and I was heartbroken. I didn't know what to say or how to encourage him. Grief was setting in, in the form of silent tears. I didn't want my father to focus on me; I needed to focus on him at that moment. My tears could wait. So now I've taken my notes, interactions, and hospice volunteer experience over the years to write this book that focuses on the terminally ill person and their needs instead of the survivors'.

It's difficult to see your loved ones deteriorate before your eyes but imagine how they feel to see themselves become weaker, not able to do for themselves. Their mind is telling their body to act, but the body is not responding. You may dread caring for a family member, but they may dread it even more than you, and it can manifest itself in misdirected anger at you and you at them. Both people are hurting, but one has to check their anger, and, unfortunately, it's often the one who's suffering. Or they just push everyone away.

The burden of needing someone to help them do the simplest of things, like going to the bathroom, bathing, getting dressed, and feeding them, can be humiliating. Now add the family member's murmuring and complaining over having to take care of them, making them feel like a burden. It adds to their physical pain and the reality of their illness.

Grief doesn't just affect those who suffer a loss, it also affects those diagnosed with a terminal or life-limiting illness. They go through similar stages as well and need support from family and friends. So, let's look at how to support, encourage, and listen to family and friends who have been diagnosed and give them the support they need.

Life-Changing Diagnosis

T he doctor sat her down, cleared his throat, looked at her chart, then back at her as he spoke. "Is there any family with you?"

She shook her head.

He nodded and continued with the diagnosis.

Her eyes widened and her heart raced at the words pancreatic cancer. She felt as if something had just sucked the life right out of her.

Shocked, she murmured, "pancreatic cancer. Are … are you sure?"

The doctor just nodded his head slowly, while watching her intently as the color drained from her face.

"It can't be! This can't be happening to me. Doctor, are you sure?" Her hands were starting to shake.

"Yes," he assured her, "stage 3. I'm sorry." He handed her a tissue for the tears that had started to fall. "Is there someone I can call for you?"

She shook her head. "No, I'll be alright. I just need a minute."

He stepped out for a moment and then returned with a woman, his assistant, and continued talking about the disease and treatment options, but she found it hard to focus. She was numb from the news, trying to wrap her head around his words, but they seemed so foreign.

This type of situation happens too often. Loved ones receiving life-changing news must take time to process what they have been told. The shock of hearing you have a life-limiting disease or terminal illness that could end your life much sooner than you could have ever imagined is heartbreaking. You can't believe it; you think there must be a mistake. No one wants to hear that they have years, months, maybe only weeks to live. How you wish you could do the day over again and skip going to the doctor. But now you're forced to start seeing life differently, while in the back of your mind you're hoping it's all a mistake or bad dream.

Just like the woman portrayed above, this scenario resonates with quite a few people. All your health concerns over the past several months have finally been diagnosed. It's not the news you wanted to hear. In an instant, your world has been turned upside down, or you feel like the rug has just been pulled out from underneath you. For a while, finding solid footing will seem tricky, and quieting your imagination will take some work. We always picture the worst and then stay there without noticing it until it starts to consume us.

BE PROACTIVE

There's nothing wrong with getting a second opinion. Being 100 percent sure will help you figure out your next steps. Ask questions about your illness and take lots of notes. You can even use a recorder to make it easier and more accurately remember the answers, especially if you are by yourself. Find out all you can about how it will affect your quality of life and the symptoms. Attend support groups in your area. It's never too early to connect with other people with similar diagnoses. Death isn't always imminent, and knowledge is empowering even when facing death or a significant life change.

You will experience several waves of emotions during this time. For example: a loss for words, numbness, not wanting to talk about it or anything else. Don't beat yourself up or allow others to make you feel guilty. Your responses may be similar to someone going through the stages of grief. This is not uncommon, and people need to be aware that you might experience different types of loss over a period of time within yourself. It's only natural for your emotions to feel as if they are spinning and taking you with them.

You are the one who needs to be sure that you get the care and support you need to make the most of your life and the best decisions going forward. People will sympathize with you, and some may even empathize, as they have gone through or may be going through some type of illness. Still, no one will know exactly how you feel because they are not you. Some people are stronger than others when it comes to dealing with crises. Others may be able to stay more positive or get back up right away and keep moving ahead regardless. If you are not that type of person, this doesn't make you weaker. You just need to make sure that you get the support you need in and/or outside the home.

There are five phases to be aware of when being diagnosed with a terminal illness. Not unlike the grief phases, they will give you an idea of what to expect as you walk this path. These phases are not absolute or exact. Each person is unique; however, these phases will help you understand what usually happens and how it can affect you. The Terminally Ill Phases chart below will help you understand what you can expect.

TERMINALLY ILL PHASES

1. The first one is called the *Initial or Pre-diagnosis phase*. In this phase, a person may experience changes in their body like aches and pains or just an overall feeling of not being well. You know something isn't right because of the symptoms you're experiencing. However, in this

phase a person may also know that a certain disease or illness runs in their family and seeks a medical diagnosis thorough examination and testing to confirm or deny their suspicions.

2. The *Acute phase* is when you have an answer to the question "What's wrong with me?" or your suspicions have been confirmed. Now it's time to discuss the type of illness you have. You'll want to know if it's terminal, what stage you are in, and how long you have to live. You'll want to know if it's treatable, what your options are, and what effects /side effects you might experience in your body. If there are experimental treatments, consider them carefully. Understand that aggressive treatments may kill cancer cells but also harm healthy cells too. You decide what treatment is best for you. After all, you're the one who has to endure it!

3. The *Chronic phase* can last months or years, as it has more to do with adjusting to the diagnosis of your illness—not to be confused with chronic illness, as in reoccurring, acute, or the length of time you've had the illness. The doctor diagnosed you with an illness and now you have to adjust to the news. If it's a slow progression, and you may not be receiving treatment, you may question the diagnosis. This phase can recur over and over again with a disease like dementia, which affects the thinking and memory daily. The person may forget that they have dementia, and when they remember, the stages of grief—anger, denial, and

depression—may start all over again. It can also happen with other illnesses, especially when treatments work well so that you forget that you're sick. Or you start feeling better after a short period of time and start wondering if the diagnosis was accurate.

4. The *Recovery phase* is not about recovering from the illness. After months or years of agonizing over your diagnosis, you've come to terms with what it means and how it can and will impact your life. Emotionally you have recovered from the highs and lows and grief. There may be moments, but they are few and far between. You're strong enough to not become overwhelmed like you were in the past. You're armed with knowledge about what you're dealing with. Think of it as recovering your life and then making the best of it.

5. Last is the *Terminal phase*. You're in the final stages of the illness or disease. You may be in the hospital, hospice, or your home. The treatments you receive now are to make you as comfortable as possible. In this phase, as with the others, you still matter. Breathe your last breath on your terms if possible. This can be expressed in your final wishes. Spend your days with loved ones or in quiet reflection. Regardless of the time you have left, don't spend each day wondering if this is it! Because you might just look back and realize that you have been asking that question for the last six months to a year or more. (for more information see... Five Phases of Terminal Illness (healthcare-information-guide.com)

NOTE TO THE FAMILY:

Having your loved one diagnosed with an illness that could take their life is a lot to take in. Your life and others' may be greatly affected and changed. The thought of one day losing a parent, child, or sibling can be overwhelming. Just as you were not prepared to hear the news, neither were they. They don't have any answers and don't know what to expect in the future.

They may reassure you, but try to be the one to reassure them. Find ways to support them in the days ahead. Do research with or for them. If possible, go with them to the doctor's office. Allow them to be upset, and resist the urge to give them motivational speeches that are not motivating. They will need encouragement, but timing is key. "I'm here for you" is one of the most important phrases you can say and mean. Allow them to tell you when, where, and how they will need you.

Processing What You've Heard

Taking a deep sigh, he stared off into the distance searching for an answer, a silver lining, or at the very least some hope. Water always brought peace and rejuvenation when facing a storm in his life. But the cool breeze coming off the lake did nothing to calm his fears.

His eyes locked on a cloud passing by. "What should I do now? How can I fix this? Is this even real?

"What to do? What to do?" He rubbed the sides of his head because his temples were now throbbing.

The rowboat kept bobbing up and down like his emotions.

"How do I tell my family? Argh." He groaned and threw the paddle down in the boat.

He had been diagnosed two weeks ago, and the last thing he wanted to do was upset his family. Every chance he got he'd slip away to the lake. Here, many problems were solved through quiet reflections and silent conversations.

Unfortunately, this time, after many hours and finding no answers, he sighed again and started paddling back to shore.

———— · ～◇～ · ————

Are you confused and unsure of what to do next? Now that you have been diagnosed, you're probably finding it hard to accept. It's okay to feel at a loss. Take time to gather yourself and process what you've been told. Being diagnosed with a terminal illness has delayed and even changed the path and plans of your life beyond your control. You will have to reevaluate your life and adjust when and where needed. However, you don't have to do it at that moment. Stop trying to work things out as soon as you leave the doctor's office.

Not everyone's disease progresses at the same pace. Some stages might be longer than others. You may go into remission or be cured. Maintaining your focus will be a challenge. Try to think of the best person to help you focus because your mind will be fixated with fear and anxiety for you and your family. How will this disease affect them? If there are children, how will they handle the news? If you are single or a single parent with no family and friends to turn to, this may be even more difficult to handle. This is when support groups and/or a counselor will be beneficial to you from the very beginning.

You will have treatments and doctor visits that will take priority over everything else in your life, as well as financial concerns, medical bills, final arrangements, and so much more. Support from family, friends, and religious groups will be especially important. First, take the time to acknowledge your feelings concerning this disease before considering others. Process what you've heard so that you can begin to move forward to get what you need during this time of adjustment. Burying your emotions and ignoring the diagnosis will only bring more pain to you and others.

Please understand, as I said earlier, that you will also go through stages of grief—not just your family. If you are young, not being able to look forward to the future will feel unfair. Not seeing your children grow up or grandchildren being born can make you feel robbed. Not getting married or getting to grow old with your spouse is depressing. You might feel cheated out of life while wondering "Why me?" There will be so many fears and thoughts that it will feel overwhelming at times. If you are a caregiver, you may worry about who will take care of the person in your charge when you no longer can.

I remember a woman at my church who was taking care of her husband, who suffered many health challenges including cancer. He was always in and out of the hospital. She was very energetic and smiling. She didn't consider her husband a burden because she loved him so much. I'm sure she had moments of weariness and anxiety about him dying, since they were both up in age and living alone.

One day she fell ill and shortly after that died, to everyone's surprise. The husband's spouse/caregiver was suddenly gone. She had preceded him in death, and he was left to deal with not only his illness but the loss of his wife. This happens more often than we realize.

It's not uncommon for families to be dealing with multiple illnesses at one time. In the time of COVID-19, some families have been devasted by an unexpected loss on top of terminal illness, while other families have suffered multiple losses one after another, leaving them very little time to grieve. People have had to alter their lives quickly to fill in the voids left by those whose lives ended without warning. In situations like these, sometimes the processing comes after the loss, not before.

It's never easy to hear words that can change the direction of your life unexpectedly. Don't allow others to pressure you into acting contrary to how you feel. You have to process and not just react. The choices and decisions you make in the beginning will be some of the most important ones and can affect you greatly.

When it comes to figuring out the next step, take time to get the information you need to be better informed about what you are dealing with. Stop, take a deep breath and then keep moving forward. You are alive right now! So, decide to live every moment on purpose even in the midst of sadness.

If you are a take-charge person, then that's what you need to do to give your life normalcy. Your peace comes in having as much as possible set up ahead of time, especially if others depend on you. If those are adults, they will need to learn how to become self-sufficient. This will give you greater peace in the end.

NOTE TO THE FAMILY:

Your loved one needs time to process the news they have heard and what it means. They are no different than you when trying to wrap your head around their illness and disease. Resist the urge to ask them a lot of questions that they may not have answers to right away. Instead, write down your questions and ask them at a more appropriate moment and you might only get a couple of questions answered at a time. Also, the answers may come without you having to ask.

First, just take the time to consider how they must be feeling and be there for them. Instead of asking them, "What are you going to do?" just let them know that you are there for them and they don't have to figure things out today. Support them right where they are—no questions. You usually know the type of person they are, and this can help you in helping them.

Some people are the take-charge type and want to start figuring things out, especially with words like Stage 4. Sitting still is not an option for them. Idle time sends their mind into fear, anxiety, and worry. Allow them to do whatever they need to while offering your help, even being proactive. This means that you may not have time to process what you've heard, but it's important that you find time, even quiet moments, to assess your feelings as well.

If, however, they are not the take-charge type, you or someone may have to step in and help them to focus on daily tasks. Don't plan their life for them. Give them every consideration in all you do by making sure it's what they want and not what you feel they need. Remember, you taking the lead doesn't mean they have no say.

How Do I Tell Them I Might Be Dying?

Her head was spinning trying to decide who, when, where, and how to let her husband and children know that she has Huntington's disease. She hoped and prayed that she would not inherit the disease her father died from five years ago.

"Mom." Her voice was low and trembling.

"Yes, sweetheart," her mother said, sitting by her side, holding her hand. Her eyes were filling with tears, but she held them back for her daughter's sake.

"I'm scared." She wiped the tears as they started to fall faster. "I knew this could happen, but why now? Why me? Jeremy is only three years old. Grace is only six. I don't want them to see me falling apart right before their eyes, and I don't want to forget them." Her voice rose with anxiety.

"I know, I know," her mom said, squeezing her hand tighter. "But I'm here for you, and I'll be here for Michael and the children as well."

At that moment she remembered all that her mother had gone through with her father and the disease. Her heart ached even more. "Mom." She began to sob. "I'm sorry. I'm so sorry you have to go through this again," she said, forgetting about herself.

Her mother reached over and began gently wiping her tears. "Don't you worry about what I went through with your father. It was hard, but I'm better prepared now to help Michael, the children, and especially you." Trying to reassure while wrapping her arms around her. "I think we should tell Michael first. Remember, he was around during your father's illness and knew that this could happen," kissing her on the cheek.

"I know, but if it had to happen, I just hoped it would be when the children were at least in their teens or graduated from high school. I just ... I just ..." Her voice cracked between the tears. "I just wanted them to have good mem-mor-rieees." She was now crying uncontrollably.

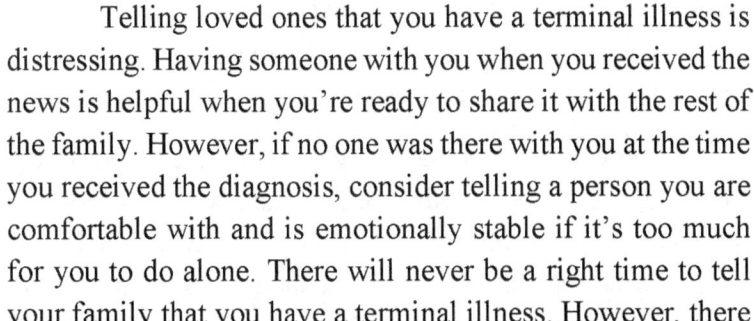

Telling loved ones that you have a terminal illness is distressing. Having someone with you when you received the news is helpful when you're ready to share it with the rest of the family. However, if no one was there with you at the time you received the diagnosis, consider telling a person you are comfortable with and is emotionally stable if it's too much for you to do alone. There will never be a right time to tell your family that you have a terminal illness. However, there may be a time more suitable than another to share your life-changing news.

This will be one of the hardest things you'll have to do, next to seeing yourself deteriorate and those last days of saying good-bye. Knowing how you felt when you were told may make you consider not telling anyone, but you have to. You can tell them individually or all together, or, as noted earlier, you can have someone help you deliver the news. Know that their reactions will vary from shock and disbelief to hugs, tears, anger, and even silence. They too will have to deal with you having a terminal illness and how possibly losing you will change their life while preparing to live without you one day.

However, you may not feel like saying anything to anyone at all because you're having a hard time accepting it yourself. Shock and disbelief are where you are until you come to terms with the diagnosis. Still, you must come to terms with it sooner than later. Saying nothing can have a devastating effect on the family, especially if they find out when your illness takes a turn for the worse and you pass weeks or days later. It can also cause harm and tear the family apart with accusations that someone knew and didn't tell, especially in blended families and second marriages.

I knew of two situations where this happened. In the first one, the husband didn't tell his family of his terminal illness and kept pushing himself until the disease took its toll on him. He was rushed to the hospital, where the family found out about his cancer. He never left the hospital. This was a blended family; his children couldn't believe that his wife knew nothing about his illness even though the children had been around him as well.

The second situation involved a husband who firmly stated that he didn't want his family or his wife's family to know about his illness. So, she honored his request even though she would occasionally gently suggest that he should reconsider and at least tell his family. Nonetheless, he didn't and eventually died. His family was so upset with her for not telling them that it caused a major rift in the relationship. To tell or not tell is a weighty decision to make, but understand that when you're gone, the consequences fall on those left behind and can tear the family apart.

Instead, consider making a video or writing a letter to those left behind of your decision to keep your illness a secret. It should come from you in one form or another. To leave the burden on someone else is selfish and inconsiderate. Your family should at least know that it was your choice and why. This won't ease their pain and they may still get mad at the other person for not telling, but it will let them know that it was your choice!

NOTE TO THE FAMILY:

When your loved one finally tells you about their diagnosis, just know that they are dealing with a lot. It's okay to be sad, mad, or angry, but, remember—they are the ones who will actually go through physical, emotional, and mental pain and suffering as their illness progresses.

For right now, while they are with you, focus more on them, and make the most of the time you have with them. It may feel unfair, but they feel the same way about the diagnosis and the helplessness they will experience as their body and maybe their mind changes. Depending on the illness, they may not always be around, and you can't get back any time lost. Being a burden is the last thing they want to be to others. So don't treat them as if they are a burden. Help is available if needed; please seek it out if necessary.

Putting on a Brave Face

G ood morning. How are you feeling today?" she asked, fixing his plate. "How did you sleep?" "Not bad. I watched movies all night. I think I overdid it. I'll get some rest after breakfast," he answered without looking up from his smartphone.

He had stayed in the den all night with the TV on to cover his occasional groans because of the pain and not wanting to worry her. He also spent most of his time worrying about her and how she was handling everything since he was no longer able to work. Some days were good, but most days were starting to become bad. He was hurting most of the time, and his pain medication made him tired and sleepy.

"Well, there must have been some good shows on to keep you up." She laughed, setting his plate in front of him, and sat down. But she noticed he was occasionally biting his lip and shaking his leg constantly as if he was in pain.

"It was okay. I slept off and on through most of them," he said, forcing a smile. "After my nap, I'll mow the lawn."

"Oh, I forgot." She stood and quickly ran off. A few minutes later she came back with his pain medication, "You should take these with your food." She set the pill bottle next to his juice and continued talking about random stuff.

Our body has a built-in defense mechanism that helps us to cope with stressful situations. Too often a terminally ill person will neglect their emotions and needs in order to help others. This is a defense mechanism to keep themselves preoccupied from their approaching death while hoping for a cure or at least remission. They will usually try to maintain daily routines for as long as possible until they just can't do it any longer. Family and friends need to allow them this as long as it doesn't cause stress or harm to themselves or others. They need to maintain a lifestyle of normalcy to help them cope.

If you're the terminally ill person, you'll feel the need to put on a brave face to ease your loved ones' pain and sadness. You'll insist that everything is fine and that you're dealing with it. You'll do your best to encourage them, especially if you have children or a spouse. If you're not careful, you'll bury your pain to ease theirs, and that will only add unnecessary grief and stress to your mind and body. Don't burden yourself with the grief of others. Allow other friends and family members to help them and focus on you. This is not easy to do, but it must be done; if not, you'll only wear yourself out sooner.

Men are good at hiding their emotions to protect their loved ones. It is harder for them to share their feelings and may take them longer to talk about their illness or even tell their families. They have to try to figure things out before they do. They're used to fixing problems, and when that ability has been taken away, they feel helpless, frustrated, and angry at not being able to do anything. If they are the breadwinner, they may become consumed with the well-being and security of the family.

We've all heard that "real men don't cry"—but they do! They have to release the pain and frustration, even fear, so they can continue on. Don't allow society's norms or even what you have been told by the older generation of men in your family to force you to suffer in silence. Your emotional well-being is just as important as anyone else's. Sadness and grief are gender neutral. They don't care whether you are male or female, young or old—everyone suffers. The only difference is how you handle, process, and go through your illness.

So, cry if you need to. Find a quiet place where no one is around if you must and yell, scream, sob, ask God why! Whatever you need to do to release the tension and anxiety you are feeling. If not, you might just release it on your loved ones instead by snapping at them or shutting down and closing yourself off from your support system. The same goes for women as well.

Children, on the other hand, usually show a wide range of emotions when dealing with a terminal illness. Confusion and fear of the disease are usually the first emotions to surface. They will have a lot of why questions as they try to understand the look on your face and others'. They are usually very vocal with their concerns because they will want to know why Mommy and Daddy are sad or about to cry.

They too will put on a brave face so that you won't be sad. They will try to comfort you and tell you everything will be okay.

One of the good things about children is that they will usually tell you how they feel when asked. If they don't know the words, they may say, "I don't feel well" or "It hurts" and tell you where or point. They will have both up and down moments as the disease progresses. Parents are generally good at keeping themselves together for their child. They will keep their grief in check and find quiet moments away to break down before pulling themselves back together.

Also, adults have a way checking their emotions in front of children. They will usually break down when the child is asleep or not close by. Their whole focus is making the most of the time their child has left. Trips to Disney and other things the child may want to do will be granted, if possible, to bring them as much joy as they can. All adults usually feel a need to make a child happy in the midst of their disease and don't find it a burden to do so.

However, teenagers will be quite different. They are aware of death and have a greater understanding of their disease progression when explained. They are more prone to shutting down and like adults will have a roller coaster of emotions and responses. They can and will snap at people because of fear and anger. Try not to take it personally. They are trying to deal with something bigger than they are and scary. Even though they are a teen, they still have limited experience handling their emotions and expressing their fears. Children and teenagers will go through the grief process, just as adults do. Be patient and understand that they are doing the best they can to manage their emotions and the disease.

NOTE TO THE FAMILY:

Your loved ones will try to convince you that they are okay when they're not. Depending on your relationship with them, you will have to pay attention to their facial expressions and body movements for pain cues. Let them know that it's okay to feel bad and rest or take their medication even if it makes them sleepy. They will usually overdo things to not be a burden when they are tired or have no energy or strength. Just because they say they are okay, it doesn't mean they are. The brave face is for your benefit, as they are making sure that you are okay, or they don't want to worry you. Regardless, just as they are concerned about you, you should be concerned about them and their well-being.

The Breakdown

Lynn and Janet sat on the patio in silence. They had been friends since elementary school and shared everything with each other, including the good and bad times. Now in their fifties, Janet's terminal illness threatened to separate them permanently.

Lynn noticed that Janet was becoming more withdrawn and was worried about her. She reached across the table, placing her hand over Janet's. "It'll be alright."

Janet snatched her hand away and turned to Lynn with a look of fear and despair. "I'm dying. How will that be alright?" she replied angrily.

"No, I mean that I will be here for you, that you are not alone," Lynn quickly answered.

"No, I am alone in this! No one but me is suffering, and no one but me is going through chemo, and no one but me is losing weight and hair and in excruciating pain. I'm the only one going through these dreadful changes—no one else."

As she struggled to stand, she looked over at Lynn and said, "I know you mean well, but I'm tired of people offering me sympathy or pity. I'm not getting any better, only worse. I'm trying to come to grips with dying, and I don't want false hope or encouraging words. I just want to be left alone for a while until I decide it will be alright!" She turned and slowly walked back into the house.

The last thing you want to hear when you're sick is "it will be alright." I'm dying—how will that be alright? you think, if you don't say it out loud, out of shock, anger, or frustration. You may be envious that others will continue living or angry because it's not fair. The words cancer, leukemia, MS, Parkinson's or whatever your diagnosis is has left an open wound. They don't understand how it feels to have your whole life stamped with an expiration date. The last thing you want to hear is anything positive or encouraging.

Unfortunately, when people don't know what to say, they tend to say the wrong things. They mean well, but some of the things they say makes no sense. Usually, their words are more for themselves than for you. They're still processing how their life will be without you. You're the one suffering, and they will be left to pick up the pieces and fill in the void of losing you.

Then there are times when no matter what a person says you will not receive it well. Where you are at with dealing with your diagnosis matters in how you receive and respond to others. However, try to handle your emotions in a way that is not abusive to others. They may be hurting, and your words may push them away and cause a wedge that you think you don't care about, but you do care.

We have all heard the saying "Hurting people hurt people." It's true people act out of pain and fear. They are so focused on their death that they forget to live. They don't recognize the love of others, and they struggle to see tomorrow. Everything has become tainted because of their illness. However, you who have been diagnosed may have to fight to keep fear and negative thoughts at bay. Fight to live and not become overwhelmed with death.

When we think of grief, our thoughts will immediately go to the loved ones who will be left behind. Rarely do we think about a person dealing with a terminal illness. However, they are suffering loss on a continuous basis from the diagnosis to death. Every time they hear a bad report or lose a faculty or body function, it can be distressing and depressing, and they grieve. What they experience is called preparatory grief.

Preparatory grief can be experienced in the terminal stage. It can also happen as soon as a person is diagnosed and told there is no treatment or cure. The person grieves as they realize that death is imminent. So, they do their best to adjust to their physical changes and emotional anxieties in their own time. It is inevitable as they go through the dying process.

In the beginning is shock and disbelief at the diagnosis. Denial may lead them to get a second or even third opinion, hoping for a different outcome. They may become angry with God, doctors, themselves, or their family genetic history for their getting sick and isolate themselves from everyone else. They bargain with God to heal them. They may feel guilty about dying and leaving loved ones behind, especially their children. They become depressed and feel a sense of hopelessness and helplessness to change the outcome. At some point, hopefully, they learn to accept their diagnosis and focus on making the most of their time or situation.

The grief that family and friends usually experience while their loved one is battling an illness is called anticipatory grief. *Anticipatory grief* is experienced by the family and friends as they struggle with thoughts and feelings surrounding the future loss of their loved one. It can also be experienced by the person dying as they are anticipating their death, degrading mentally, or developing physical incapacities.

Either way, everyone deals with an impending loss in their own way. Grief is a natural process of loss that we experience. People want to help; they want to do something to ease your pain and add joy to your life. So, when they see you're grieving, they feel compelled to do something, and it's okay to tell them what you need and don't need. It'll help them help you.

I encourage you to focus on your health and well-being and not the illness. You can still be the healthiest version of you in the midst of sickness and disease, starting with your mind-set. Self-care is important. Instead of focusing on the negative, count your blessings for what you do have. What you did achieve. The loved ones surrounding you, including friends. Also, if your body permits, get a massage and pamper yourself to the degree that you can.

NOTE TO THE FAMILY:

The grieving process cannot be rushed. It takes time to accept that death is occurring and to work through feelings that arise as a result. The individual going through these grief processes may ultimately experience a transformation from profound sadness to a sense of comfort. They may be sad all the time. They may even be angry and unbearable.

It's hard not to take it personally, especially when you are the only one willing to be around them. However, it could be the medication, anger at the disease, or a sense of helplessness that is affecting their mood. Their behavior is not okay! You may have to seek help in caring for them.

Either way, try not to treat them the same way they are treating you. It's okay to step back if you need to.

Also, take the time to care for yourself. Find time to do little things that make you happy and relax. You can get a massage to help release tension. Go for walks, a drive, whatever it is that will give you a moment of peace. Do it for your loved one, and it may also help their mood.

I said this because taking time for yourself can make a positive difference. It can make others feel better and less burdensome. They genuinely wish to see you happy and engaged. Also, sharing your experiences when asked about your day can strengthen your connection with them. Plus, your experiences might inspire and motivate them in their own lives.

Cry, Cry, Cry!

R ichard sat in his favorite chair facing the fireplace. He was deep in thought when he felt something roll down his cheek. He didn't bother reaching for his face because he knew exactly what it was—tears! This was becoming more frequent every time he was alone and deep in thought. His mood was becoming melancholy even though he tried to act more alive than half dead.

This time, however, not aware that anyone else had entered the room, he noticed a box of tissues with a sticky note attached. He knew immediately who had placed it there: his sister, the optimist. A kind person, she would always say, "Our emotions don't show up when it's convenient; they show up to let us know how we are feeling."

The sticky note read: "Use me in times of light or heavy rain."

He laughed and cried at the same time.

Whoever said "Big girls don't cry" or "Grown men don't cry" lied to themselves and everyone else. Tears have nothing to do with how mature you are. There's nothing macho about denying your feelings to keep up appearances. Men especially are taught to respond in a non-sensitive way so as to not be seen as weak or soft. This train of thought benefits no one and hurts everyone involved. What's more important is not how others see you but taking care of yourself and learning to release the pain in a way that helps you cope with the changes in your life.

Crying doesn't make you pathetic; it's your body's way of dealing with emotional or physical pain. It helps to alleviate stress and frustration. Stifling your tears will not help anyone, especially you. Our tears are a natural response and aren't meant to be shown just when it's convenient for others. Crying can be good for us and help us feel better. It's also a way we show others how we feel. We cry sometimes when we are happy, so why is it any different when we are sad?

Life is not always about convenience, and it shouldn't be. It's about being honest with yourself and others, not putting on an act out of fear of what people will think. It's more natural to cry than not to cry. Everyone cries sometimes or at least sheds a tear. Your life has changed in a way that you may not fully understand, and the uncertainty of what's next can and will have your emotions all over the place. It's okay to cry as you redefine your life in the midst of sickness and disease.

Break away and have a good cry if necessary. Then pull yourself together and keep going. No one has to know unless you share it. Also, seek out family, friends, or a support group that you can be vulnerable in front of, knowing that they will keep you protected by respecting your privacy and pain. Don't keep the heartache/heartbreak inside. You will never begin to get what you need if you do. No one can read your mind, so don't expect them to.

Now, if you are crying incessantly, all day every day for an extended period, it might be wise to seek professional help. When diagnosed with an illness, depression can set in as one grieves and constantly thinks about dying. Fear can also trigger depression, which can lead to another set of health challenges and even suicide if left unchecked. Death is final, and the thought of that can be disheartening and cause anxieties.

Again, don't feel guilty about breaking down—it's natural and necessary. Your loved ones should allow you the space to do so. Don't worry so much about upsetting them with your tears or making them sad. Most of the time they will not mind, and you usually know the ones that will. Emotionally strong family and friends are usually better at supporting you through those moments.

Also, it's okay to say, "I don't want to talk right now." As death becomes imminent, this may be the case. You may spend more time alone, bedridden and not feel like talking much. This doesn't mean you don't want to see anyone; you may welcome a quiet visit. Your loved ones need to know this. They can sit with you in silence, holding your hand, quietly reading to themselves or to you, or even daydreaming. Their presence is what you'll cherish, and no words are needed except "I love you." A touch communicates a deeper connection than words ever can. It says, "You mean more than the world to me," and it can be felt.

More importantly, your loved ones need to know that you can't be positive every single moment of the day.

NOTE TO THE FAMILY:

So, family, let them cry, get angry, or be quiet. Give them the space to deal with their emotions in their own way. I know that it can be hard to handle their emotional breakdowns but remember you're not the one going through what they are. Show compassion! If their emotions are too much for you to handle, separate yourself before you become hostile toward them. You may be in the anger stage at the disease and taking your frustration out on your loved one, which will only add to their pain.

They are looking for a safe place to be vulnerable with their emotions. What they are not looking for is twenty questions or what you think they should do. They want support and need your patience as they are learning to deal with a major curve ball that has caught them off guard. They will have to rethink many areas of their life and redefine other aspects of their life to accommodate changes in health. This means that, for a while, they might be self-absorbed and distant in thought. Don't take it personally when they have to work through some things on their own.

On the other hand, you might have a family member who will rely on you for everything. This happens with people who are used to someone else doing everything for them. They have never had to make a crucial decision in their life. This person will usually give someone else all the control and just do what they are told. They may even be more fragile both emotionally and mentally. As a result, you may feel as if an enormous weight has been placed on your shoulders. Get help! Don't beat yourself up if you can't do it. Find support from family members or a social worker. You don't have to do it alone.

Just Let Me Know You Care

H is avoidance was obvious. He rarely spent time in the room as he always found something that needed to be done or would murmur a few words and leave.

She found herself dealing with two kinds of pain: physical and emotional. The pain brought on by the disease and the heartache of feeling alone. The second was more mental, as her mind tried to measure the distance that was increasing between them. She and her husband were struggling to deal with her dying as their love had become buried beneath the illness. As they struggled to deal with disappointment, her fear became clear.

The nurse had just left the room a few minutes before he came in. He stood there just looking at her lying in bed and shook his head.

The lights were dimmed because her eyes had become sensitive to bright lights.

"Is there something you want to say to me?" she asked, breathing heavily.

"What are you talking about?" he replied knowing she was right. Something was on his mind and had been for a while.

He glanced around the guest room she now occupied because of all the equipment and special bed she needed. The smell reminded him of a nursing home and seeing her with tubes was more than he could handle. She seemed so thin and frail. This was not the life he wanted and taking care of his wife had become nerve-wracking.

"Don't you think it's time you considered going to a facility to get the care you need?" His face flushed with embarrassment. "I don't mean to sound cold, but this is more than I can handle and unfair to me," he murmured.

"Unfair to you?" she asked, attempting to sit up. "Are you serious?" She paused, angry and hurt by his words. "How is my illness unfair to you?" She spoke slowly. "I don't see you hooked up to machines and an IV pole," pausing again to catch her breath. "I don't see you struggling to breathe, remember things or having to rely on others because you've lost your ability to do for yourself. You can come and go as you please, enjoy your life, and plan for your future." Her face had now turned red, and she was becoming winded again.

He just stared at a corner of the room to avoid eye contact. His wife had become a stranger to him. He no longer felt love for the woman he had once planned to spend his life with; instead, he felt only guilt for wanting her out of his sight. It was difficult to look at her because the disease had ravaged her body and reduced her to skin and bones. Her hair was gone, and her eyes were now sunken in. She looked more like an old woman clinging to life.

After a minute or two she continued. "I'm sorry if my illness is inconvenient for you, but it's not like I planned to become ill." Her eyes were becoming glazed. "I had plans for my life too, and now I have no future. I live day to day, never knowing what the next few hours will bring." She laid back staring at nothing.

Her voice was now barely audible as she spoke. "I thought that at least my husband would be here for me if no one else would." She closed her eyes. The conversation had left her broken and her heart shattered. The fear that she had tried to keep at bay was now overwhelming her, and she had no desire or energy left to fight it. Her face was wet with tears, and she felt more alone now than ever before. Darkness closed in on her as she took her last breath.

Her husband just stood there unaware that she had died.

———— · ⟁ · ————

No one wants to die without knowing that someone cares. It doesn't matter whether it's family or friends. Even the angriest, most frustrated, hurt, scared, or fearful person wants and needs someone by their side. The thought of dying can make a person unbearable, miserable, and say hurtful things, but it's still fear. Even people who have for years kept others at a distance still wished they had someone who cared but may have been scarred by disappointment and hurt.

I remember when I was a hospice volunteer, I saw a person who grumbled at everyone, turned away anyone trying to be nice. He would often say, "I don't want or need anyone's pity or help" or "I don't like people." So, people avoided him and did very little for him. Still, I saw how he looked when other people had visitors, and they were happy. For a moment something in his eyes wanted that for himself before he shook it off and started complaining or left.

No matter how bitter a person is, most people at some point in their lives want to know love. Other times a person may feel as if they haven't accomplished anything and are afraid of being forgotten. This usually happens with people who have no friends or family. No one comes to visit, which for them means no one cares. This is especially hard for people with family members who are indifferent toward them. A person may feel as if they have been cheated because they are not ready to die. They dread missing out on life because now they realize it was worth living.

Unfortunately, some relationships fall apart because the other person can't handle the physical and emotional changes they or the other person is experiencing. This adds to their anxiety of being abandoned, resulting in broken hearts for both the person dealing with the illness and their loved ones. The last thing they want to do is become a burden on the family.

On the spiritual side, not knowing what's after death scares people. They wonder if there is a heaven or hell. Which one will they go to, if either? Most people want to live longer and grieve dying too soon. Especially if they feel as if they haven't fulfilled their purpose or destiny. Life is a gift that some find they've wasted or didn't appreciate.

NOTE TO THE FAMILY:

As I said earlier, no one wants to die without knowing that someone cares. Usually, they may have a certain person they need to feel this from: a husband, wife, children, parents, siblings, or friends. One person's love may mean more than others', and when they don't get it loneliness or abandonment issues can set in.

Fear can affect anyone at any time, including the person who is dealing with sickness and disease. It's almost impossible to not feel some type of anxiety with a wide range of emotions. The same way you would be there for a child dealing with a sickness is the same way you should be there for an adult. They may not have the words to express themselves, but you can see that they are struggling. No one expects you to have the answers or know what to do, but being there for them is one of the most important things you can do.

Your loved one has issues they are battling. They may not be able to share them because they are trying to understand what's going on. Their life has just changed in a way that changes everything they have ever known, and your support is crucial even from a distance. When they lash out, forgive them and try to understand that they are attempting to wrap their head around the possibility of dying.

If you are finding it hard to deal with their illness, admit it to yourself and them and step aside. If not, it will soon become evident as time goes on. This may lead them to be more determined to hide their feelings or information about the progression of the disease.

It doesn't mean that your feelings are not important—they are—but now is not the time to burden them with your concerns. Find another family member or friend to share with if you need to. In the meantime, give them as much love and support as you can.

Pain, Pain, Go Away!

I lay in the hospital bed rocking back and forth in pain. The doctors couldn't give me anything strong because it would affect my bowels, and that was the problem. My bowel obstruction was serious, and I was angry for being sent back home in pain from the ER because they missed it. Now a tube was shoved up my nose to pump my stomach.

"Can't you please give me something for the pain?" I asked, almost begging.

The nurse just shook her head. "I'm sorry, but anything stronger will relax your bowels, and we don't want that to happen." Her tone was sympathetic but didn't take away the pain.

I glanced over at the pump removing the waste from my body and sighed.

"What am I waiting for?" I said, shifting in the bed, hoping for a less painful position.

"We have to clean your system out and hope that your bowels open up on their own," the nurse answered.

That didn't happen, and four days later came the surgery. It was a success, but the pain remained—just not as strong.

With my eyes lifted, I said, "God, I'm tired of this. I can't do it anymore. I'm tired of hospitals, surgeries, IVs, needles, and most of all pain!"

I had hit a wall, and I had no strength or desire to go through any more possible health challenges in the future. At that point, it didn't matter whether I lived or died just as long as I didn't go through anything else. A few friends who came to visit could tell that I was numb and maybe indifferent.

I didn't care what people thought, and I didn't care if I closed my eyes and didn't wake up.

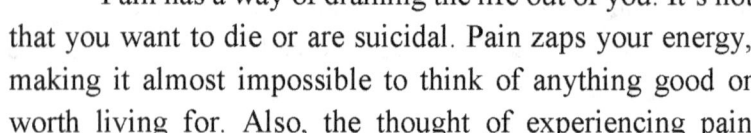

Pain has a way of draining the life out of you. It's not that you want to die or are suicidal. Pain zaps your energy, making it almost impossible to think of anything good or worth living for. Also, the thought of experiencing pain almost every day of your life is not appealing. You can't walk, sit up, or lie down for very long because it hurts in any position.

You want the pain to end, and you're tired of taking drugs. No one understands how you feel. Some people may be able to empathize with you, but they're not you and that's the difference. You can't get your loved ones or even the doctor to understand what you are going through. You don't care how other people have coped; all you care about is you and how you are coping. You can't focus because your mind is blank, and everything said is meaningless if it doesn't address the pain.

Yelling is usually a natural response to people who just don't get it. You're frustrated with everyone's thoughts and opinions. You want to be left alone because the aggravation is causing your pain level to rise. Or you suffer in silence because you don't want to worry others. Or smile around people and cry yourself to sleep, if possible, because you hurt so much. Relief—it's all about relief, and if the pain persists for months or years dying doesn't seem so bad if it's the only way it will stop.

Telling people how you feel is not always to get them to understand. Sometimes it's about just telling them how you feel with no expectations they will understand. Just say, "This is how I feel." That's it! Oftentimes you'll feel like you're in a corner by yourself. It might be true, but that doesn't mean that you shouldn't share what you're going through with someone. Occasionally what matters most is not being understood but being heard.

The pain doesn't always go away. Life can seem unfair because of your suffering. Is there something positive in all this? Will things get better? The answers aren't black and white. Each situation is different, just as each person is different. The way you get through the pain depends on you.

It's not about being weak or strong. Be true to yourself and figure out what coping method works best for you.

NOTE TO THE FAMILY:

When someone we love is dying, it can be hard to let go. We want them to try every new or experimental drug on the market in hopes that one will work. After a while, they can become tired and don't feel like trying any more treatments. They may be in pain, tired, and just want release, but all we see is our need for them to stick around.

Too often our thoughts can become self-centered. You can be blinded by love or fear if that person is your strength or took care of everything. It's easy to neglect or ignore their pain because of your anxieties. However, don't ignore their feelings. If things are not getting better, don't expect your loved one to suffer by refusing to let them go because you're not ready. Don't hold on to them or try to make them feel guilty for not wanting to take or try anything else.

Look at them and remember that they are the ones taking drugs or going through these sometimes painful treatments. They are the ones getting poked and prodded, throwing up, being operated on, and who knows what else hoping something will work. So, when they say, "I can't do this anymore," or "I'm tired," resist the urge to accuse them of giving up—especially if it's been years of battling the disease.

Finally, resist the urge to compare your past pains and how you dealt with it to theirs. You may have a high tolerance for pain and they don't, or vice versa. It's their body and they know when they have reached their pain limit. It's easy to say "keep fighting" or "don't give up" when you are not the one experiencing it.

No matter what happens, they gave it their all. They fought to live and not die. They did all they could. Their body took all it could take before they got to the point of saying enough is enough, I can't do it anymore. It might not seem like it was enough to you, but it was enough for them. Accept that they've had enough, and choose to support them to the end.

Life Changes

Dear Diary,

I have not completely come to terms with my illness. My heart is broken, and I don't know where I'm going to find the strength or if I want to. My family tries, but they don't understand. My future involves the grave much sooner than I had hoped.

I've asked, "Why me?" so many times, but I know there's no answer to the question and none that would make me feel better or give me peace.

I have to learn to accept the things that I can't change, or so this placard on the wall called "Footprints" tells me.

What if I don't want to learn to accept the things I can't change? I want to change things. I want to live longer. Am I wrong …?

I guess I have no choice because this disease is changing me from the inside out. Everything has changed. Nothing is as planned. When I look in the mirror, I'm changing, getting smaller. Then again, I said that I needed to lose weight. Ha ha ha!

They say, "Laughter is the best medicine." Can laughter heal me? Can it take away the cancer that has invaded my body?

No, it can't! I guess it only makes life bearable at times.

When I allow myself to laugh, for a moment I forget I'm sick and I'm light in heart. Maybe that's the magic of laughter. It injects joy in the midst of pain to ease the heartache.

I'm tired now, and my thoughts are becoming scattered again. At times I feel as though I'm in a fog and the words are floating around me, but I can't catch enough of them to make sense to others.

I realize that I have to find a way to continue for as long as I can. It's not easy, but I don't want to just lie down and die either!

Today was a good day. I hope tomorrow will be too.

Signed: Alive while Dying

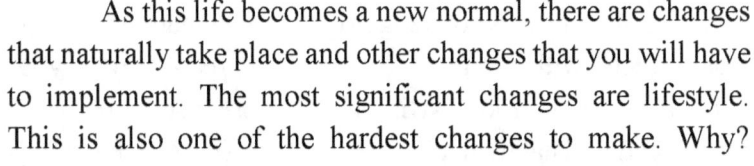

As this life becomes a new normal, there are changes that naturally take place and other changes that you will have to implement. The most significant changes are lifestyle. This is also one of the hardest changes to make. Why? Because most people need normalcy in their lives to function and to be able to cope. Too many changes too fast can cause stress and resistance even if they are needed.

You need time to adjust and refocus before moving your life in a new direction. Evaluate where you are in life. Do you need to create new dreams and goals that are realistic to your situation? Your priorities may have changed, but then again maybe not. Some people who never thought about life and goals will suddenly realize there are things that they want to accomplish or see. A type of bucket list will be helpful.

Others will be forced to take a long, hard look at their disease and prepare for the long road ahead. If that's you, stay optimistic for a cure or remission. Don't give up hope that life can be better than before but different. Fight to save your life by doing what's necessary, and that starts with learning all there is about your illness. Knowledge is power and helps you create a better quality of life no matter the time span. It also helps you help others support you in a way that benefits you the most.

Relationships can be strengthened when there's knowledge about the illness and possible limitations. Also, communication is key to helping others involved in your care. Your family won't have to guess whether you're having a good or bad day. Knowledge of your medications and the side effects will help you and others realize that your irritability and mood swings are not just you being disagreeable. That will also help others to not take things personally and help your doctor make changes, if necessary, to your medications.

At some point, there are things you will have to start to consider, like writing a will if you don't already have one. Who will be your (durable) power of attorney in case you're unable to make decisions on your own? Even planning your funeral and where you want to be buried might be something you need to consider. Some people find solace in doing these things for themselves, while others may find it too disturbing. One way or the other, do what makes you comfortable.

Be as explicit as possible with your wishes and care. This will help the person or persons you've chosen to make decisions on your behalf. Also, it will cut down on confusion and in-fighting among family members. While you are alive, delegate responsibilities so everyone knows their roles. Assign a caregiver—they don't have to always be a family member. They can be a close friend or from an agency. Whoever is capable of making decisions that benefit you that you trust.

Now is also the time to prepare your children for life without you. If you're the type of parent that did everything for your children, there'll be a tremendous amount of worry and concern about their future. Your adult children who fall in this category will have to learn to be self-sufficient. You can help them by encouraging them to start doing things on their own. If you're in the early stages of the illness, are in remission, or are cured, this should be a wakeup call that you need to take a less active role in the lives of your adult children.

However, if you are dealing with a terminal illness with no cure, then you need to wean your adult children off quickly but still help them to stand on their own. This not only will help them but give you peace as the illness progresses. Every parent wants to know that their children will be alright without them. You're no exception! Give them more responsibility for their own care, and help them to work out solutions to their problems. This doesn't guarantee their success, but it won't hurt their chances. With or without you, they'll have to move on and do for themselves unless they just start to depend on someone else.

Below is a sample checklist to consider as you plan the next phase of your life.

- Create a will (if you haven't).

- Select someone as your Durable Power of Attorney.

- Decide whether you want to be resuscitated. If not, you'll need to sign a DNR (Do Not Resuscitate).

- Create a bucket list of things you would like to do in the time you have left.

- Plan your funeral/burial site.

- Gather all your insurance policies, bank books, stocks, 401k, IRAs, and anything else in one place so it's easy to find. Include instructions on how to access all your accounts (passwords, user ID, etc.). Also, make sure your insurance policies and bank accounts have a beneficiary listed.

- Delegate responsibility to those capable of carrying it out, including your care at home. Before you become too ill to act or talk, have this conversation.

- Make a memory book, cards, or videos for each of your loved ones as gifts.

- If you have family members who depend on you, like the elderly or children, now is the time to have a backup plan of care for them when the time comes.

NOTE TO THE FAMILY:

While terminally ill people can start making life changes after their diagnosis, another thing that might suddenly change is getting in touch with their spiritual side. Some people become spiritual, while others rely heavily on their relationship with God. If this is what makes the illness bearable, then don't try to take it from them. Don't tell them they're being foolish or to snap out of it. Faith for some plays a major role of support.

Don't steal their hope and peace because you don't agree or understand. It is important to listen to the dying person's needs and not impose your fears, beliefs, or preconceived notions on that person.

Remember, you're on the outside looking in, viewing life from your perception and beliefs. If you don't have any beliefs or agree with theirs, don't argue or criticize them. You don't want that as part of your last words and memories with them. Also, it wastes precious time. Even if you have been through a similar situation with your health, you're not them and they're not you, and that's the difference.

Also, people's priorities change, and things that were important before their diagnosis may no longer be. They haven't given up; they just see other things as more important. Short-term goals are easily achievable and may take precedence. They have reevaluated their life and found a prospective that matches where they are at right now.

They may sound as if they have given up because they are planning for their death by getting things in order, but they are not. They are being proactive in their life by making decisions that affect the time they have left. So, be patient and supportive. You may be surprised at the renewed purpose they've found.

We're in This Together

C heryl walked into the craft store to pick up some yarn. She looked around, happy to be in her favorite store but feeling overwhelmed at the thought of having to walk around and push a cart without getting tired. There were no carts to ride in so, she just took a deep breath and started moving forward.

About five minutes down the center aisle, she mumbled, "Why is the yarn always in the back of the store?"

Normally, she would have already been in the yarn section and had at least two skeins in the basket. These days she felt as if she moved slower than a turtle.

She finally made it to the yarn aisle but needed to rest. Maybe this wasn't a good idea. I should've just ordered online.

Knitting was one of the few joys left in her life that didn't zap her strength, and she could go at her own pace. After a few minutes, she felt a tap on the shoulder and turned to see Maria, one of the store's employees, standing beside her.

"Hello, Cheryl, it's been a long time. It's good to see you again. We've missed you." She smiled.

"Hi, Maria, I know. I missed shopping here too! Today is the first day in a long time that I've actually had the energy to shop," she said, sounding breathy.

"Oh, Cheryl, you sound winded. Are you okay? Do you need anything?" Maria looked concerned. Cheryl had been one of their faithful and loyal customers for many years. They were unaware that she had been sick.

"No, I'm fine. I just need a minute to rest."

"One moment, I'll be right back," Maria said and quickly walked away.

After a minute or so she returned with a stool. "Here, sit down. Today I'll be your personal shopper," she said, clasping her hands together and laughing. Tell me what colors you're looking for, and I'll bring the yarn to you and anything else you need.

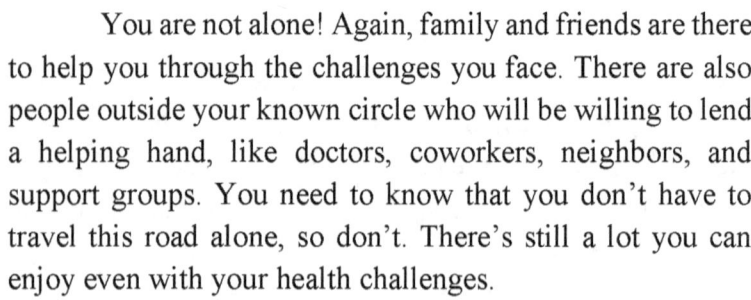

You are not alone! Again, family and friends are there to help you through the challenges you face. There are also people outside your known circle who will be willing to lend a helping hand, like doctors, coworkers, neighbors, and support groups. You need to know that you don't have to travel this road alone, so don't. There's still a lot you can enjoy even with your health challenges.

You don't have to give up on happiness or doing some of the things that brought you joy in the past. With better planning and help, you can still get out and live your life with minimal boundaries. There may be a time where you will need to scale back or stop completely, but until then, keep going! Once that happens, find new things to enjoy within your limitations. People are willing to help out, so speak up!

If you need a hug, ask for one. Don't be afraid to ask for what you need and want. Perhaps you don't have any family, or you're not close to anyone, or they couldn't care less what happens to you. If you have family dynamics that are distancing or dysfunctional, don't despair—your support can come from others. A support group, religious group or a good friend can fill in the void most of the time. They don't have to be blood related.

Also, let people help you by running errands, doing chores—whatever you need to have done. Don't consider yourself a burden on those who want to help. It's their way of showing how much they love and appreciate you. They can't take away the illness or your pain, so they busy themselves trying to make your life or the time you have left as comfortable as possible.

You can take back control of your life. Don't give up! Take things in stride because your life still has purpose and meaning. Sometimes you can feel as if it doesn't matter even with friends and family around. You may also feel like giving up. I experienced this with my father. It wasn't that he didn't care about his family, he was just tired of pain and loss and resigned himself to dying. Let me say this: he didn't want to die; he just believed that's where his life was headed. I thank God he is still with us today.

He still struggles from time to time. Being alone is something he now has to get used to since his wife died. Although he has friends and family checking on him, it doesn't take away the pain of a loss or the digestive issues and severe arthritis, COPD, or the possibility of cancer returning. In situations like this, it's hard to not give in to the thought of dying or wanting to die. However, my father knows that he has support, and it helps him to know that he's not alone.

That's why it's important to stay connected to the people who care about you—a support group or just one person. Share how you are feeling, even if it's not upbeat or positive. If you're in pain, say so. If you're feeling overwhelmed, let someone know. Whatever it is, share it to get the help you need, and be honest about your feelings. Don't go through the illness alone. Don't think, "I'm dying, so it doesn't matter!" It does matter and you matter to your last breath or renewed health.

NOTE TO THE FAMILY:

Having a loved one or friend dealing with a terminal or life-limiting illness can be challenging. You may feel like you're walking on eggshells sometimes with their emotions. You may want to stay clear of them because of their mood swings or yours with having to care for them. Your life can seem to stand still. If you are their caregiver, it's even more draining on you mentally, emotionally, and physically. The same can be true with caring for elderly parents.

Still, you must find time for yourself. Consider scheduling a time of refreshing for yourself by asking other family members to help. There are also other resources like home health aides, CNAs, and agencies that can step in to give you a break. Don't let family members or other people make you feel guilty for needing a regular break. It's just as important for you to take care of yourself so you can be there for others.

However, now in the time of COVID, it's hard to get out, and you're careful about who you let in. It makes things more challenging but not impossible. Take a drive or a short walk for your break or anything else you may want to do. Someone may be willing to stay with your loved one for a few hours. You'll never know unless you ask. In the meantime, cherish your loved one because tomorrow is not promised to any of us.

Valarie Lovelight

Common Struggles

The instructor was a middle-aged woman with salt-and-pepper hair. She was sitting off to the side watching people find seats. The room felt cozy instead of sterile, and about twenty-five people had signed up. Forty people could have easily attended, but she wanted breathing room for those who wanted a little more space.

As it was now ten minutes before class was to start, she got up and individually greeted those in attendance. "Hello, my name is Leslie—welcome. I'm glad to see you here this evening." This she did right up until the start of class.

Walking back up to the front, she said, "Thank you all for taking the time to attend this class on managing your emotions. The reason we ask for the family and patient to attend together is so that you will be better prepared to help one another. Friends are also encouraged to attend as they may sometimes find themselves in the role of offering caregiving support from time to time."

She opened her manual. "Some illnesses are slow in progressing, giving people time to wrap their head around what's going on. Other diagnoses progress much faster, sweeping families up in a whirlwind." The instructor motioned with her hands.

She began to talk about common struggles. "Let me say this: during the course of the illness, you may not realize that what you are feeling the other person might be feeling too. For example: frustration and fatigue. These are two of the most common shared emotions between caregivers, family members, and patients. All parties have to realize that emotions like these will strain relationships if boundaries are not set.

"First, understand that your caregiver can get frustrated and tired. There are no age considerations—young and old can feel this way. And you as the patient don't own the exclusive rights to these emotions."

There were nods of agreement, looks of confusion, and heads shaking in disagreement. One person asked, "How can your caregiver get frustrated? Why should they be frustrated? If it's their job, then they should know how to manage their emotions. That's what they are getting paid for, so I don't think they have the right to feel that way." Others agreed with the comment.

"You're right," said the instructor. "A caregiver that comes to your house from an agency has a set time to come and go with specific tasks to do for their patient. Even then, patients and their families can be overly demanding and rude, leading to frustration, and your caregiver quits." She chose her words carefully.

"However, when caregivers are family members, they tend to be on call all day long. Expected to stop what they are doing every time the patient, their family member, needs something, and their life is put on hold. They don't feel like they have time for themselves, and that can be frustrating and tiring. If they're getting paid, then they're only required to work the hours they're getting paid for. This doesn't always work, so there has to be a compromise to allow both people to get what they need, including personal time."

One woman quickly spoke up. "This is true. I've experienced this with both my parents. I have siblings, but they're too busy with their families and work to help out. At times I get so mad and frustrated that I end up yelling at my parents because I'm tired, and it's not their fault. I wish my siblings would help out more and realize they are not the only ones with a life.

"How has that affected the relationship within your family?" the instructor asked.

"I get angry and not wanting to be bothered with anyone. My siblings think because they call or stop by a few times a month or give a couple of dollars that they are doing their part." Her eyes started to water. "It's not my parents' fault, and I can tell that they feel guilty having me care for them. They're always apologizing or trying to do more on their own. It's not hard caring for them. I just need a break—

and more than a couple of hours. I need a couple of days or a week." She accepted the tissue box that was handed to her.

"Caregiving isn't easy, because it requires time. This is why you should get help from an agency, if possible. If you don't qualify for free assistance, there are agencies that can still help you. Hospice agencies have volunteers, your church or religious group members are sometimes willing to help out, and consider calling foundations that deal primarily with the person's type of illness to see what's available," she said, stepping out from behind the podium.

"There are also financial struggles that can add stress to any situation. For example, money for medicine or to pay bills if the person can no longer work due to their illness. But, also, for the caregiver that's a family member. They may end up losing or having to leave their job to be a caregiver. It may start out as temporary, but depending on the level of care and lack of support, it can become long-term. Now both people are worried about finances, including keeping a roof over their heads and food on the table."

The instructor noticed a young woman who looked like she wanted to say something but kept hesitating.

"Excuse me," said the instructor to the young woman. "I can see you want to say something—please share your thoughts. This class is designed to help everyone get some insight, vent, or share what's on their mind."

The young woman looked around, cleared her throat, and spoke. "I care for my mom and I love her, but sometimes she makes me feel like I'm obligated to care for her."

"What do you mean by obligated?" the instructor asked.

"She always says how she raised me and took care of me growing up and that I have my whole life ahead of me to live, so I shouldn't complain about wanting to do things because she needs me. I don't hate my mom, but I'm starting to resent having to take care of her because she wants my life to revolve around her, and if anyone else tries to help me out, she complains about every little thing they do to make me feel guilty." Tears were running down her face.

The instructor handed her a box of tissues. "If I may ask, how old are you?"

"I'm thirty-two years old."

"Is your mother terminal?"

"She's in remission and doing much better. There are still things she can't do for herself and other things she can do but doesn't bother to try. I think she's just gotten used to me doing them for her."

The instructor nodded in understanding. "Sounds like codependency."

"Codependency?" the young woman repeated.

"Yes, you have given up a lot of your time to help care for your mother in her time of need. Which is commendable. But it seems as if she has become dependent on you always being there and now depends on you for even the things she can do herself," she explained.

"Oh, I understand." She sighed.

Placing her hand on her shoulder, she said, "I know what that feels like; I experienced that with my own parents when they were alive. The people we care for not only are afraid but also have comfort zones they don't want to leave. Unfortunately, their need for comfort can and will encroach on our life and invade our freedom. To say something makes us sound thoughtless and insensitive to what they are going through."

"You're right. If I say something, she calls me selfish and says I'm only thinking about myself," the young woman responded. "Sometimes I just want to go out with friends. I'd also like to go out on dates. I don't think that's selfish of me. She's in remission, and if she lives another five, ten, or twenty years—which I hope she does—does it mean I have to put my life on hold for that long? It's not fair for her to be sick, but it's also not fair for her to expect me to stop living because she might die one day."

"It sounds like you both need counseling or else your relationship will continue to deteriorate. We can talk after class about options for you to explore, especially for yourself."

A woman in her forties raised her hand to share. She had a scarf tied around her head and looked very tired and thin. "I don't want to be a burden on my family. I don't think anyone wants to be a burden on others. Sometimes I do feel like I'm asking too much and I try to do some things on my own, but I feel like it's not enough. Even coming here was a challenge for me because I walk slowly."

She paused to gather her thoughts, "My family is very supportive, and sometimes when I need help, I don't ask for it. Especially if I feel like I've asked for so much already. I will wait even if it's something I really need, like pain meds, or go and get them myself if the pain is really bad. Cleaning up a mess I made sometimes results in a bigger mess." She stopped to cough. "If I see someone starting to get frustrated with me, I stop asking and get quiet."

Her husband was sitting next to her and reached over and wrapped his arms around her and spoke directly to her, "You are not a burden to us, even if we seem frustrated, busy, or tired. That's still no reason for you to suffer in pain or not ask us for help. This cancer has all of us feeling dazed, but you mean the world to us, so don't you forget that. We will be alright regardless."

Everyone listened intently as others shared their experiences—some good, some bad, and some heartbreaking.

Whether you are a caregiver, a family member, or the person living with a life-limiting illness, it's common to have different levels of emotions and feelings. What we need to remember is that each person will have good and not-so-good moments that will require them to regroup physically and emotionally. They will experience some of the same emotions but from different perspectives.

Here are some common struggles that both the terminally ill person and family members and friends deal with:

- Trying to find the right words of comfort and encouragement.

- Not having enough money for treatments, medicine, burial, food, bills, etc.

- Trying to avoid negativity. If you are dealing with an illness, you don't want tears or people talking as if you're dying tomorrow. As a family member, you don't want to hear your loved one constantly talking about death and dying.

- Struggling to find a bright side to life.

- The shock of diagnosis, which leads to questions, sadness, and speechlessness.

- Coming to terms in their own way.

- Reckless behavior, depression, and suicidal thoughts. Thoughts of dying/the thought of losing someone you love. Parent(s) who have lost a child suddenly, especially to suicide, may experience this type of behavior.

- Struggling to find the meaning in anything. For the patient, losing the ability to walk or think or losing limbs. For family, the thought of losing the person.

- Feeling nothing matters anymore! This thought can affect anyone, not just the patient.

- Worrying about the family, and how those left behind will manage, especially if the dying loved one is the breadwinner.

The key to dealing with struggles is to realize that most of them are commonly shared. The caregiver may not be able to empathize with the person who is suffering, but they can understand a common feeling. For example, you're scared of dying, and they're scared of losing you—different sides of the same coin called fear. Another example is fatigue. As the person with the illness, your medication and overall disease progression can leave you tired and exhausted. For the caregiver, picking up the slack in household chores, shopping, cleaning, and taking care of you while working can leave them just as tired and exhausted, and if they wake up in the middle of the night to care for you, this adds to their tiredness.

Struggles remind us that we are human; we can't do it all and need help. There's no shame in reaching out to other family members and friends or even a health-care agency.

Instead of becoming divided and combative with each other, use these commonalities to increase greater awareness of each other and extend grace and understanding. Wisdom dictates that we walk in love, and for some it means taking the higher road because not everyone will agree on common struggles or see them as shared emotions.

People dealing with an illness that affects the mind like dementia or Alzheimer's will not remember, agree, or notice. Others will be so into their own pain and disappointment that they don't care about what you're going through, especially as a family member/caregiver. If that's the case, then it's up to you to make sound decisions for your health and sanity so that you don't become angry and indifferent toward them.

The most important thing to remember is the love! Heartaches and disappointments are real and will leave you depressed, especially if you only focus on the past or the things left undone. Even though you have been given a diagnosis that has now altered the trajectory of your life, the biggest change you must fight against is not allowing it to destroy your heart and love. You'll have to battle negative emotions and resist the urge to fall into the pit of despair.

> *Remember: your illness doesn't have to rob you of everything. There are still people who love and care about you because you are worthy of being loved and cared about.*

NOTE TO THE FAMILY:

Common struggles are real between all involved. It's easy to get frustrated and snap at the people around out of frustration, exhaustion, and resentment of feeling as if your life has been put on hold. Your loved one may seem clueless as to your feelings and not having a personal life. If you're an adult (child) or other family member, the person suffering may feel they've done so much for you, you shouldn't have a problem taking care of them.

It's times like this where you might have to seek outside help for both you and them. But understand that while the person you're caring for might seem selfish, having strangers care for them might be scary. Especially if they're limited in their ability to care for themselves. They may be concerned about being abused by their caregiver or taken advantage of.

This is usually why they reject having a stranger in their home having access to their personal information. Scenarios like this are more real than many people know. If they are reluctant or overly disagreeable, don't just pass it off as them being stubborn or trying to ruin your life. It may be more, so pay attention. It's okay to get what you need as long as you don't sacrifice your loved one in the process.

Everyone can become frustrated working through emotions and fears. No one owns exclusive rights to feeling a certain way—not the caregiver or person diagnosed.

Communication is key in learning to maneuver your way through the ups and downs of any illness. Your patience will be tested and your love. Try to always see your loved one through the frustration. Remember, they are trying to do the best they can in finding the positive in a heartbreaking situation just like you.

Illness shouldn't divide us; it should bring us together. Common struggles can be a bridge that connects us together to weather the storm that any sickness and disease can and will bring.

Don't Forget to Bloom!

When thinking back over our lives, we realize there are some things we would change if possible. Those things aren't always bad—just some adjustments that would have made our lives a little easier, or at least so we believe. Hindsight could benefit all of us in some way if it were possible. But we don't have pre-vision or the ability to change things in our past. No one does.

It is said, "Live your life as if every day is your last day." Or "Tomorrow is not promised." These saying are true. We don't know what tomorrow holds or even what will happen today. We plan our lives as though there will always be a tomorrow, knowing for some, today might be their last day, hour, or minutes.

However, life is meant to be enjoyed as much as possible. We are to live to the best of our ability a full life with very little regrets and leave behind beautiful memories for others to remember us by. Fragrances of joy, peace, happiness, and love for others to draw strength from especially in times of hardship, sadness, and sorrow. Although, it's not always possible, because people's lives aren't perfect.

Sickness and disease have a way of making themselves known at the most inconvenient times and causing fear, anger, and depression. Lives are altered in the blink of an eye with no way of knowing what's next, how things will change, or the impact it will make. But do all you can to stay strong for your loved ones and most importantly for yourself. Find a way to push through the negative emotions, depression, fears of the diagnosis, and illness itself. I encourage you to get the help and support you need to make the most of your time regardless of the illness.

Bloom in the midst of sickness and disease no matter the season. All flowers have a time and season to grow, bloom, and wither away. Even some weeds serve a purpose in the ecosystem, though other weeds are like a cancer that grows and overpower what's around it and must be removed from the root in order to preserve the plants surrounding it.

The flowers around it don't give up. They continue to do what they were created to do: grow and offer up their beauty and fragrance. Don't you give up. And, whenever possible, offer up your beauty and fragrance for as long as possible. Please understand that it comes from the inside, not the outside. Your appearance as your illness progresses has nothing to do with the fragrance you give off to those around you. So, live your purpose to the end, and don't forget to bloom in the season you're in so others will have a fragrance to remember you by.

Moment of Reflection

L ife is like a handful of threads woven together to make an intricate pattern. Sometimes those patterns can be complex or simple, long, or short. Each piece is unique to the designer as he chooses the tools to create what he believes is the best for him. However, there's always a chance that he may run out of thread before he is finished. Or the thread may break during the process, leaving the work unfinished.

Still, each piece is beautiful in its own way. Unfinished works are just as precious as finished works. Truth be told, most works go unfinished. The designer can always add more and rarely seems satisfied. Such is life, for we never seem to accomplish all we want to do regardless of how much time we have or what we have already done. There will always be one more task, goal, project, or finishing touch!

No matter the season … don't forget to bloom!

Organizations and Resources

1. American Psychological Association - www.apa.org/pi/aging/programs/eol/organizations

2. Simpli - www.simpli.com/people/uncovering-hidden-costs-budgeting-paying-family-caregivers

3. www.simpli.com/lifestyle/receive-financial-support-family-caregiver

4. www.caregiver.org

5. Community care programs and services (varies by state, county, and community)

6. Dream Foundation - www.dreamfoundation.org

7. Association for Death, Education and Counseling - www.adec.org

*Your doctor can also provide a list of resources for your illness.

Acknowledgments

For those who have touched my heart and opened my eyes and mind to the other side, this process has been a labor of love. It would not have been possible for me to complete this project without my parents' love and support. Having the opportunity to volunteer at Hospice of Michigan and meet patients and fellow laborers taught me unconditional love in the face of sickness and disease.

Thank you to my family and friends for constantly encouraging me to keep sharing hope, love, patience, and longsuffering with others.

About the Author

Valarie Richardson (Lovelight) is certified with the American Caregiver Association (ACA). Her volunteer experiences include Hospice of Michigan and various hospitals over the years. Being up close and personal with families in their time of need through her work in pastoral care has broadened her view of life, death and dying. It doesn't matter how small the impact may have been, every tear shed by someone or heartbreaking phone call has contributed to shaping her.

On a lighter note, she enjoys drawing, watercolor, reading different genres and poetry. In her spare time, she crafts and shares it with others. She spends her time between New Jersey, Michigan and occasionally Germany.

www.ingramcontent.com/pod-product-compliance
Lightning Source LLC
Chambersburg PA
CBHW070441130626
46553CB00006B/2274